Mitchell C. Henderson

THE ULTIMATE GUIDE TO ESCAPING THE BROKE LIFESTYLE

PRACTICAL STEPS TO STOP LIVING PAYCHECK-TO-PAYCHECK AND BUILD FINANCIAL FREEDOM

The Ultimate Guide to Escaping the Broke Lifestyle: Practical Steps to Stop Living Paycheck-to-Paycheck and Build Financial Freedom

Copyright © 2024

All rights reserved.
No part of this book may be reproduced in any form without permission, except brief quotations for review purposes.

ISBN: 9798304124065

Disclaimer:
This book is for educational and motivational purposes only. It does not constitute financial advice. Readers should consult a qualified financial advisor before making financial decisions.

This book is dedicated to everyone out there who was born broke but wants to break free!

Contents

Introduction *Why "Broke" is a Mindset,
Not Just a Bank Balance* 7

Chapter 1 *The Real Cost of Living
Paycheck-to-Paycheck* 10

Chapter 2 *Common Traps That
Keep You Broke* 14

Chapter 3 *The Emotional Side of Money* 19

Chapter 4 *Budgeting Made Simple
and Effective* 24

Chapter 5 *Building Your Emergency Fund* 30

Chapter 6 *Getting Out of
Debt for Good* 36

Chapter 7 *The Power of
Small Investments* 42

Chapter 8 *Redefining
Needs vs. Wants* 47

Chapter 9 *Increasing Your
Income Without Burning Out* 53

Chapter 10 *Financial Systems
That Work for You* 59

Chapter 11 *Planning for the Future* 65

Chapter 12 *Giving Back and
Building Legacy* 72

Conclusion *Breaking Free is a Journey,
Not a Destination* 78

Bonus Materials
   Worksheets, Reflection Questions, Resources 82

Introduction

Why "Broke" is a Mindset, Not Just a Bank Balance

Picture this: Two people are standing in the same field, staring at the same patch of dry, rocky soil. One sees nothing but an impossible situation—no crops will ever grow here, so why bother trying? The other sees potential, grabs a shovel, and starts clearing the rocks, knowing that with hard work, seeds, and a little rain, they'll eventually harvest something great. The difference isn't in the soil; it's in the mindset.

Being broke can feel like that rocky field—hopeless, overwhelming, and unyielding. But here's the truth: "broke" isn't just about what's in your bank account; it's about what's in your mind. It's the belief that your circumstances are fixed, that you'll always be stuck in the same paycheck-to-paycheck grind. The good news? Mindsets can be changed.

This book isn't about shaming you for where you're starting. I get it—life happens. Maybe you're drowning in debt, barely scraping by, or just plain exhausted from working hard and feeling like you have nothing to show for it. That's real, and it's tough. But I'm here to tell you that you don't have to stay stuck.

The Path Forward

The journey to escaping the broke lifestyle isn't about winning the lottery or landing some once-in-a-lifetime break. It's about small, consistent steps that lead to big, life-changing results. It's about reprogramming the way you think about money, creating habits that work for you, and taking control of your financial destiny one decision at a time.

By the end of this book, you'll have:

- A clear understanding of how the "broke cycle" works and how to break free from it.
- Practical tools to budget, manage debt, and save money—even if you think you can't.
- Strategies to grow your income and start building wealth, no matter where you're starting.
- The confidence to stop surviving and start thriving financially.

This isn't a quick-fix, get-rich-overnight kind of guide. It's a blueprint for lasting change—change that starts in your mind and ripples out into your bank account, your future, and your life.

Your Wake-Up Call

Here's the thing: no one's coming to rescue you. The government, your employer, even your family—they can help, sure, but ultimately, your financial freedom is in *your* hands. That's a scary thought, but it's also empowering. Because if it's up to you, then you have the power to make it happen.

Right now, you're standing in that field, staring at the soil. You have a choice to make: will you focus on the rocks or grab a shovel and start digging?

Let's dig.

Chapter 1

The Real Cost of Living Paycheck-to-Paycheck

The Silent Weight of "Broke"

Living paycheck-to-paycheck feels like running on a treadmill that won't stop—no matter how fast you go, you're not getting anywhere. It's exhausting. And the cost isn't just financial. It weighs on your mental health, strains your relationships, and keeps you stuck in a cycle that feels impossible to break.

Financial stress is one of the biggest causes of anxiety and depression. You're constantly worrying about whether you'll make rent, keep the lights on, or afford groceries. It keeps you up at night and robs you of peace during the day. But the toll doesn't stop there. It spills over into your relationships, causing arguments, mistrust, and sometimes even resentment.

Then there's the opportunity cost. When every dollar is spent just trying to survive, there's nothing left for building a better future. You miss out on investing in yourself, saving for emergencies, or saying "yes" to opportunities that could improve your life.

The Hidden Costs of Debt and Instability

Living paycheck-to-paycheck comes with a price tag you don't always see. For one, there's the high cost of debt. Credit cards, payday loans, and overdraft fees might seem like lifelines when you're short on cash, but they quickly turn into chains. Interest rates stack up faster than you can pay them down, and soon you're stuck paying for last month's groceries with money you don't have.

Then there are the late fees—penalties for not having enough to cover your bills on time. A $35 late fee here and a $50 overdraft charge there might not seem like much, but over time, they add up to hundreds or even thousands of dollars. That's money you could have used to get ahead, but instead, it's gone, leaving you further behind.

Being broke also limits your options. When you're constantly in survival mode, you can't plan ahead or take calculated risks. You're stuck making decisions based on what you can afford today, not what's best for your future. It's a vicious cycle that keeps you trapped.

What It Means to Take Back Control

Here's the truth: living paycheck-to-paycheck doesn't have to be your forever story. Yes, it's tough. Yes, it will take work. But you can break the cycle.

Taking back control starts with a mindset shift. It's about recognizing that your current situation doesn't define your future. It's about committing to small, consistent actions that will lead to big changes over time. It's about refusing to let financial stress have the final say in your life.

Imagine waking up and knowing your bills are paid. Imagine having an emergency fund that gives you peace of mind. Imagine being able to say "yes" to opportunities instead of worrying about how you'll afford them. That's what taking control looks like, and it's within your reach.

Your First Step

To break free from the paycheck-to-paycheck cycle, you need a plan. But before we get into the practical steps, take a moment to acknowledge this: you're here, reading this book, because you're ready to make a change. That's the first step, and it's a big one.

The journey won't be easy, but it will be worth it. Every small decision you make to save, budget, or pay down debt brings you closer to the financial freedom you deserve.

This chapter is your wake-up call. The cost of staying broke is too high, but the rewards of breaking free are life-changing. Let's get to work.

Chapter 2
Common Traps That Keep You Broke

The Invisible Chains of the Broke Lifestyle

Breaking free from financial struggle starts with recognizing what's keeping you stuck. Too often, it's not just the big financial hits but the small, sneaky traps that quietly drain your resources and keep you spinning your wheels. These traps can feel normal, even inevitable, but identifying them is the first step to escaping them. Let's call them out for what they are.

1. Living Beyond Your Means: The Lifestyle Inflation Trap

Ever noticed how expenses magically rise to match your income? It's like the moment you get a raise, you "need" a new car, better clothes, or a bigger apartment. This is lifestyle inflation, and it's a sneaky thief.

Here's the hard truth: if you keep upgrading your lifestyle every time you earn more, you'll never break free from the paycheck-to-paycheck cycle. It doesn't matter if you're earning $30,000 a year or $300,000—if you spend it all, you'll always feel broke.

Ask yourself: Are your expenses driven by what you truly need, or by what you think will make you happy or impress others? The truth is, real happiness doesn't come from the latest gadgets or trendy vacations. It comes from knowing you're building a secure future.

2. Debt as a Default Option

Credit cards, payday loans, financing plans—they all promise quick relief but come with long-term pain. Debt can feel like a solution when you're in a pinch, but it's often a trap.

The problem isn't just the money you borrow—it's the interest you pay. A $1,000 credit card balance can turn into a $1,500 nightmare if you're only making minimum payments. And let's not even talk about payday loans, where the interest rates are so high, it's like trying to fill a leaky bucket with water.

But debt isn't just about numbers—it's about mindset. Too often, we treat debt as the default option: Can't afford it? Put it on the card. Want it now? Finance it. This mindset keeps you dependent and robs you of financial freedom.

---

3. The Myth of "I'll Save When I Earn More"

One of the most dangerous lies we tell ourselves is, "I'll start saving when I make more money." Here's the truth: if you're not saving now, you won't save later.

Why? Because saving isn't about how much you earn—it's about how you manage what you have. If you can't set aside even $20 from a small paycheck, what makes you think you'll set aside $200 from a bigger one?

Waiting to save is like saying you'll start exercising after you're in shape. It's backward. The habit of saving starts now, no matter how small the amount. Even if it's just $5 a week, the discipline you build will prepare you to save more as your income grows.

---

4. Social Pressure and Comparison Culture

We live in a world where everyone's highlight reel is on display. Social media makes it easy to feel like you're falling behind. Your friend just bought a new car, your cousin's posting vacation photos, and your coworker's bragging about their latest tech gadget. It's tempting to keep up, even if it means spending money you don't have.

Here's the thing: comparison is a trap. You don't know what's going on behind the scenes. That person with the fancy car might be drowning in debt. That dream vacation could be financed on a maxed-out credit card. Chasing appearances will only keep you broke.

The only person you need to compete with is yourself. Focus on your goals, not someone else's highlight reel. The freedom of financial stability is worth far more than the fleeting satisfaction of "keeping up."

Breaking Free from the Traps

Here's the good news: just because these traps are common doesn't mean you have to fall into them. Awareness is your greatest weapon. Now that you see these pitfalls for what they are, you can start making intentional choices to avoid them.

Action Step: Take a moment to reflect. Which of these traps has kept you stuck? Write down one specific change you can make this week to avoid that trap. For example:

- If you're living beyond your means, create a budget and commit to sticking to it.

- If debt is your default, challenge yourself to make your next purchase in cash.
- If you've been waiting to save, open a savings account today and set up an automatic transfer, no matter how small.
- If comparison culture is your struggle, take a social media break and focus on gratitude for what you have.

Escaping the broke lifestyle isn't about perfection—it's about progress. Every small step you take to avoid these traps brings you closer to financial freedom. Let's keep moving forward.

Chapter 3

The Emotional Side of Money

Money Isn't Just Math—it's Emotions

If managing money were only about numbers, most of us would have it figured out by now. We'd spend less, save more, and invest wisely without hesitation. But money is deeply emotional. It's tied to how we feel about ourselves, how we view the world, and even how we process our past experiences.

Fear. Shame. Guilt. These emotions don't show up on a budget spreadsheet, but they have a powerful influence on your financial decisions. If you've ever avoided looking at your bank account balance or felt a knot in your stomach after making a big purchase, you know exactly what I'm talking about.

The good news? You don't have to stay stuck in these emotions. By addressing the emotional side of money, you can break free from the patterns that are holding you back.

1. How Fear Keeps You Stuck

Fear of running out of money. Fear of making a mistake. Fear of failing. These fears can keep you in a cycle of inaction, where you're too scared to move forward but can't afford to stay where you are.

Maybe you avoid investing because you're afraid of losing money. Or you're hesitant to pursue a better-paying job because you fear rejection. Fear has a way of shrinking your world and convincing you that staying "safe" is your best option.

But here's the thing: safety is often an illusion. Staying stuck in fear might feel secure, but it's costing you the future you deserve. The only way to overcome fear is to confront it. Take small, calculated steps and remind yourself that every successful person you admire had to face their fears to get where they are.

2. The Weight of Shame and Guilt

Money mistakes have a way of lingering in our minds, replaying like a bad movie. Maybe you've racked up debt, overspent on things you didn't need, or missed financial opportunities. Shame tells you that these mistakes define you.

Guilt isn't much kinder. It whispers that you're selfish for wanting to earn more or that you're failing if you can't provide everything your family needs.

But shame and guilt are liars. Your past does not determine your future. Every financial mistake is a lesson, and every misstep is an opportunity to grow. Instead of dwelling on what you've done wrong, focus on what you can do right starting today. Forgive yourself for the past, and commit to making better choices moving forward.

3. Reframing Your Relationship with Money

For many people, money feels like an enemy—something that causes stress, arguments, or endless worry. But what if you could reframe your relationship with money and see it as a tool for freedom and possibility?

Money is not evil, nor is it the solution to every problem. It's a resource, like time or energy, that you can use to create the life you want. When you start to view money as a tool, rather than a source of stress or shame, you'll begin to take control of it instead of letting it control you.

Here are a few mindset shifts to help you reframe your relationship with money:

- **Instead of:** "I'll never get out of debt." **Try:** "Every dollar I pay off brings me closer to freedom."

- **Instead of:** "I can't afford it." **Try:** "How can I make this possible?"
- **Instead of:** "I'm bad with money." **Try:** "I'm learning to manage my money better every day."

4. Small Mindset Shifts for Big Wins

The most profound changes often start with small shifts in thinking. By adjusting how you view money, you can begin to change how you handle it.

Here are a few simple shifts to try:

- **Shift from scarcity to abundance.** Instead of focusing on what you don't have, focus on what you can create. Abundance doesn't mean pretending you're rich—it means recognizing opportunities and believing in your ability to grow.
- **Focus on progress, not perfection.** You don't have to have everything figured out today. Celebrate small wins, like sticking to a budget for a week or saving $10 more than last month.
- **Adopt a gratitude mindset.** Instead of resenting money or envying others, be grateful for what you have now. Gratitude opens the door to growth and helps you make better financial choices.

Action Step: Rewrite Your Money Story

Take a moment to reflect on the emotions you associate with money. What fears, shame, or guilt have been holding you back? Write down your current "money story"—the beliefs and feelings you have about money. Then, rewrite that story in a way that empowers you.

For example:

- **Current story:** "I'll always be broke because I've made too many mistakes."
- **New story:** "I'm learning from my past and building a better financial future."

Keep your new money story where you can see it—on your phone, your mirror, or your desk. Let it remind you that your emotions don't have to control you. You're in charge now.

You Deserve Financial Peace

Money isn't just about dollars and cents—it's about how you feel when you wake up in the morning and how you see the future. By addressing the emotional side of money, you're not just improving your finances—you're transforming your life.

You have the power to change your relationship with money. Let's take the next step together.

Chapter 4

Budgeting Made Simple and Effective

Your Financial Roadmap Starts Here

If your finances were a road trip, budgeting would be your GPS. Without it, you're wandering aimlessly, hoping you'll somehow arrive at your destination. A budget isn't about restricting your life—it's about giving every dollar a purpose so you can build the future you've been dreaming of.

Think of budgeting as your foundation. You wouldn't build a house without a solid base, and you can't create lasting financial success without mastering this key habit. The good news? Budgeting doesn't have to be complicated or overwhelming. In fact, it can be simple, empowering, and even liberating when done right.

1. Why Budgeting Is Your Foundation

Most people think budgeting means giving up everything fun—like living on ramen noodles and never going out again. But here's the truth: budgeting is what gives you the freedom to spend money guilt-free. When you know exactly where your money is going, you're in control, and that control brings peace of mind.

Without a budget, money feels chaotic. You're constantly wondering, *Can I afford this?* or stressing about surprise bills. With a budget, you're telling your money where to go instead of wondering where it went.

Here's what a budget does for you:

- **It gives clarity.** No more guessing how much you're spending or saving.
- **It creates freedom.** When you budget for fun, you can enjoy spending without guilt.
- **It accelerates your goals.** Every dollar is working toward something meaningful—whether that's paying off debt, building an emergency fund, or investing.

---

2. Creating a Zero-Based Budget: Step-by-Step

The zero-based budget is one of the simplest and most effective methods. It's not about having zero money—it's about making sure every dollar has a job. At the end of the month, your income minus your expenses should equal zero.

Here's how to get started:

Step 1: List Your Income

Write down all sources of income for the month. This could include your paycheck, side hustles, or any other earnings. Be realistic—don't count on money you're not sure you'll receive.

Step 2: List Your Expenses

Next, write down every expense you have. Start with the essentials:

- Housing (rent or mortgage)
- Utilities (electricity, water, internet)
- Food (groceries and dining out)
- Transportation (gas, car payment, public transit)
- Insurance (health, car, etc.)

Then, add everything else:

- Debt payments
- Savings and investments
- Fun money (entertainment, hobbies, etc.)

Step 3: Subtract Expenses from Income

Your goal is for your income minus expenses to equal zero. If you have extra money, put it toward your financial goals—like paying off debt or saving for the future. If your expenses exceed your income, it's time to adjust. Look for areas to cut back so you're living within your means.

Step 4: Track and Adjust

Once your budget is set, track your spending throughout the month to make sure you're sticking to it. If something unexpected comes up, adjust your budget—it's a living document, not set in stone.

---

3. Tools and Apps to Make Budgeting Easier

Budgeting doesn't have to mean carrying around a notebook or creating endless spreadsheets. There are plenty of tools and apps designed to make budgeting simple and even enjoyable.

Here are a few popular options:

- **You Need a Budget (YNAB):** Focuses on giving every dollar a job and helps you plan for irregular expenses.
- **Mint:** Automatically tracks your spending and categorizes expenses. Great for visualizing where your money is going.
- **EveryDollar:** Created by Dave Ramsey, this app is straightforward and ideal for zero-based budgeting.

- **Goodbudget:** A digital version of the envelope system, perfect for managing spending categories.

Find a tool that works for you, but remember: the best budget is the one you'll actually use.

---

4. Common Budgeting Pitfalls to Avoid

As you start budgeting, it's easy to fall into a few traps. Here's how to avoid them:

- **Pitfall 1: Forgetting irregular expenses.** Birthdays, holidays, and annual bills can throw off your budget if you don't plan for them. Set aside a little each month for these.
- **Pitfall 2: Being too rigid.** Life happens, and budgets need flexibility. If something unexpected comes up, adjust without guilt.
- **Pitfall 3: Not giving yourself fun money.** A budget without any room for enjoyment is a recipe for burnout. Budget for the things you love—you'll stick to it longer.

Action Step: Create Your First Budget

This is where the rubber meets the road. Take 30 minutes today to create your first zero-based budget. Use an app, a spreadsheet, or even a piece of paper—whatever feels easiest.

Ask yourself:

- What's my total income for the month?
- What are my non-negotiable expenses?
- How much can I set aside for savings and debt repayment?
- What can I budget for fun and personal growth?

Remember, your first budget won't be perfect, and that's okay. The goal is progress, not perfection.

Your Budget, Your Freedom

Budgeting isn't about restriction—it's about empowerment. When you have a plan, you're no longer at the mercy of surprise bills or impulse purchases. You're the one calling the shots, and that control feels amazing.

This is your foundation. Every financial success you'll achieve starts with this simple, powerful habit. So grab a pen, open an app, and take the first step toward building the life you deserve.

Chapter 5

Building Your Emergency Fund

Your Safety Net for Life's Unexpected Twists

Life has a way of throwing curveballs when you least expect it—a surprise medical bill, a car breaking down, or an unexpected job loss. Without a safety net, these moments can send your finances into a tailspin. That's why an emergency fund isn't just a nice-to-have; it's non-negotiable.

An emergency fund is your shield against life's unpredictability. It gives you breathing room, peace of mind, and the ability to handle challenges without turning to debt. Let's explore why you need it, how to start, and how to build it into a fortress of financial stability.

---

1. Why an Emergency Fund Is Non-Negotiable

When life happens—and it will—having an emergency fund can mean the difference between a minor inconvenience and a full-blown financial crisis. Here's why it's so important:

- **It protects you from debt.** Instead of relying on credit cards or loans, you can use your emergency fund to cover unexpected expenses.
- **It reduces stress.** Knowing you have a safety net makes life's surprises less overwhelming.
- **It creates options.** An emergency fund gives you the freedom to make better decisions, whether it's leaving a toxic job or handling a family emergency without panic.

Think of your emergency fund as a gift to your future self—a way to handle the unexpected without derailing your goals.

2. How to Save $500 to $1,000 Quickly

Starting an emergency fund might feel daunting, especially if money is already tight. But remember, the goal isn't perfection—it's progress. Even a small cushion can make a big difference.

Here are some practical ways to save your first $500 to $1,000 fast:

1. Sell Unused Items

Walk around your home and look for things you no longer use or need. Clothes, electronics, furniture, and gadgets can add up quickly when sold online or at a garage sale.

2. Cut Back Temporarily

Look for areas in your budget where you can temporarily cut back. Could you skip eating out for a month? Cancel unused subscriptions? Redirect that money straight into your fund.

3. Pick Up a Side Hustle

Even a few hours a week driving for a rideshare service, babysitting, freelancing, or delivering groceries can help you build your fund faster.

4. Use Found Money

Tax refunds, work bonuses, or even cash gifts can go straight into your emergency fund. Treat them as opportunities to get ahead.

---

3. Growing Your Fund to 3–6 Months of Expenses

Once you've saved your initial $500 to $1,000, it's time to level up. Your ultimate goal is to have 3–6 months of living expenses saved. This bigger fund acts as a buffer for more significant life changes, like a job loss or major health issue.

Here's how to grow your fund steadily:

1. Set a Clear Goal

Calculate your monthly expenses, including housing, food, transportation, insurance, and other essentials. Multiply that by 3 to 6 months to find your target.

2. Automate Your Savings

Set up an automatic transfer to a high-yield savings account. Even small, consistent contributions add up over time.

3. Use Windfalls Wisely

Whenever you receive unexpected money—like a bonus, tax refund, or inheritance—consider putting a portion toward your emergency fund.

4. Celebrate Milestones

Break your larger goal into smaller milestones. Celebrate when you reach each one—it'll keep you motivated to continue saving.

4. Where to Keep Your Emergency Fund

Your emergency fund needs to be accessible in a pinch but separate enough that you won't be tempted to dip into it for non-emergencies. A high-yield savings account is a great option:

- **It's safe.** Your money is insured and protected.
- **It's accessible.** You can withdraw funds quickly when needed.
- **It earns interest.** Your money works for you, even while it sits.

Avoid keeping your emergency fund in cash at home or in risky investments like stocks, which can fluctuate in value.

Action Step: Start Your Emergency Fund Today

Take the first step toward financial peace of mind:

1. Decide how much you can save this week—whether it's $5, $50, or $500.
2. Open a dedicated savings account for your emergency fund.
3. Commit to adding to it regularly, even if it's just a little at a time.

Your Shield Against Life's Storms

An emergency fund isn't just a pile of cash—it's freedom, security, and confidence. It's the ability to face life's challenges head-on, knowing you're prepared.

You don't have to save it all at once, and you don't have to be perfect. Just start. Every dollar you save is a step closer to breaking free from financial stress and building the stable, abundant life you deserve.

This is your safety net. Build it, protect it, and watch how it transforms your journey to financial freedom.

Chapter 6

Getting Out of Debt for Good

Take Control and Say Goodbye to the Chains of Debt

Debt can feel like a weight dragging you down, keeping you stuck in the cycle of financial stress. But here's the truth: you can break free from debt—permanently. No matter how deep the hole feels right now, there's a way out. With a clear plan, consistent effort, and a mindset shift, you can reclaim your financial freedom and start building the future you deserve.

---

1. Understanding the True Cost of Debt

Debt isn't just about paying back what you owe. The true cost of debt lies in the hidden ways it impacts your life:

- **Financially:** Interest payments eat away at your income, leaving less for savings and investments.

- **Emotionally:** The stress of debt can cause anxiety, strain relationships, and limit your ability to enjoy life.
- **Opportunity Cost:** Every dollar spent on debt is a dollar that could have been working for you—building wealth, growing your emergency fund, or creating financial security.

When you're in debt, you're working for your creditors, not yourself. Recognizing this is the first step toward taking back control.

---

2. Two Proven Methods to Crush Debt

There's no one-size-fits-all approach to paying off debt, but two strategies have helped countless people regain financial freedom:

Debt Snowball Method

- Focus on paying off your smallest debts first while making minimum payments on the rest.
- Once the smallest debt is paid off, roll that payment amount into the next smallest debt.
- **Why it works:** The quick wins build momentum and motivation.

Debt Avalanche Method
- Focus on paying off the debt with the highest interest rate first while making minimum payments on the rest.
- Once the highest-interest debt is paid off, roll that payment amount into the next highest-interest debt.
- **Why it works:** You save more money in the long run by tackling the most expensive debt first.

Choose the method that resonates most with you—what matters is that you stay consistent.

---

3. Negotiating Interest Rates and Consolidating Debt

You have more power than you might think when it comes to managing your debt. Here are two strategies to make your debt more manageable:

1. Negotiate Interest Rates

Many lenders are willing to lower interest rates if you ask, especially if you've been a reliable customer. Call your credit card company or loan provider and explain your situation. A reduced rate can save you hundreds or even thousands over time.

2. Consider Debt Consolidation

If you have multiple high-interest debts, consolidating them into a single loan with a lower interest rate can simplify your payments and save you money. Be cautious, though—only consolidate if it truly reduces your overall costs and doesn't extend your repayment timeline unnecessarily.

---

4. Staying Motivated on Your Debt-Free Journey

Paying off debt can feel like a long, uphill battle. To stay motivated, focus on these tips:

1. Celebrate Milestones

Every time you pay off a debt or hit a significant goal, celebrate! Treat yourself in a small, meaningful way—it reminds you that progress is worth it.

2. Visualize Your Debt-Free Life

Imagine what life will look like when you're no longer carrying the weight of debt. What doors will it open? How will you feel? Keep that vision front and center.

3. Track Your Progress

Seeing your debts shrink and your hard work pay off is incredibly motivating. Use a spreadsheet, an app, or even a chart on your wall to track your progress.

4. Surround Yourself with Support

Join a debt-free community online, find an accountability partner, or lean on a trusted friend or family member who supports your goals. You don't have to do this alone.

Action Step: Start Tackling Your Debt Today

1. Make a list of all your debts, including balances, interest rates, and minimum payments.
2. Choose your repayment method: snowball or avalanche.
3. Set a realistic timeline for paying off each debt.
4. Take your first step—whether it's making an extra payment, negotiating a rate, or consolidating your debt.

Freedom is Within Reach

Debt doesn't have to control your life. It's not just about numbers—it's about reclaiming your freedom, your peace of mind, and your future. The journey may not be easy, but it's worth it. Every dollar you put toward debt is a step closer to the life you've always dreamed of.

Remember: debt is temporary. Your determination and action will last forever. This is your moment to break free and build a life where you're in control. Start today, and watch how your efforts transform your financial story.

Chapter 7
The Power of Small Investments

Planting Seeds for a Wealthier Future

Imagine planting a single seed and watching it grow into a mighty tree over time. That's the power of small investments. The journey to financial freedom doesn't require giant leaps—it begins with small, consistent steps. Even modest contributions can snowball into significant wealth thanks to the magic of compounding. The key is starting, no matter how small.

---

1. The Magic of Compounding

Albert Einstein famously called compound interest "the eighth wonder of the world," and for good reason. Here's how it works:

- **What is Compounding?** It's the process of earning returns not only on your original investment but also on the returns those investments generate.

- **How it Grows:** A $50 monthly investment earning an average 8% annual return can grow to over $75,000 in 30 years. Small amounts truly add up over time.

Think of every dollar you invest as an employee working tirelessly for you. Over time, those dollars earn more dollars, and your wealth begins to multiply.

---

2. Small Steps, Big Results

You don't need a fortune to start investing. Here are simple, beginner-friendly ways to get started:

Start with Index Funds

Index funds are a great entry point for new investors. They're low-cost, diversified, and historically provide solid returns over time. They track the performance of an entire market (like the S&P 500), making them less risky than individual stocks.

Take Advantage of Employer-Sponsored Plans

If your employer offers a 401(k) or similar retirement plan, don't miss out. Many companies offer a match—free money for your retirement. Even if you can only contribute a small amount, that match can double your investment instantly.

Explore IRAs (Individual Retirement Accounts)

An IRA is another tax-advantaged way to save for retirement. Whether you choose a traditional IRA (tax-deferred) or a Roth IRA (tax-free growth), it's a smart way to let your money grow over time.

Apps Make It Easy

Investing apps like Acorns, Webull, or Stash allow you to start with as little as $5. Many even let you invest your spare change, turning everyday purchases into opportunities for growth.

---

3. Overcoming the Fear of Investing

For many, the idea of investing feels overwhelming or risky. But avoiding it altogether is often the bigger risk. Here's how to overcome common fears:

Fear: "I Don't Know Enough"

- Start with small amounts and learn as you go.
- Use free resources like podcasts, blogs, and beginner-friendly books.
- Remember: no one becomes an expert overnight —progress is more important than perfection.

Fear: "I'll Lose My Money"
- Avoid risky "get-rich-quick" schemes. Instead, focus on long-term, diversified investments like index funds.
- Understand that markets fluctuate, but historically, they tend to grow over the long haul.

Fear: "I Can't Afford to Invest"
- Even $10 a week is better than nothing. The sooner you start, the more time your money has to grow.
- Cut back on small expenses (like coffee runs) and redirect those savings into investments.

---

4. The Long Game Mindset

Investing isn't about quick wins—it's about patience and persistence. Wealth-building is a marathon, not a sprint. The earlier you start, the more time you give your investments to grow.

Consider this example:

- **Person A starts investing $100/month at age 25** and stops at 35, letting their investments grow untouched.
- **Person B starts investing $100/month at age 35** and continues until they're 65.

Even though Person B invests for 30 years compared to Person A's 10, Person A often ends up with more money, thanks to the extra time for compounding.

Action Step: Start Your Investment Journey Today

1. **Set a Goal:** Decide on a small, manageable amount to start investing each month.
2. **Choose a Platform:** Research options like a 401(k), IRA, or an investing app.
3. **Take Your First Step:** Open an account and make your first investment—even if it's just $10.

Invest in Your Future, One Dollar at a Time

Investing isn't reserved for the wealthy—it's the tool that builds wealth over time. Every small step you take today is an investment in your future self.

Don't let fear or the misconception that "it's too late" hold you back. The best time to start investing was yesterday. The second-best time is today.

This is your moment to take control, grow your money, and break free from the cycle of financial stress. Start small, stay consistent, and watch your wealth grow—one dollar, one decision, and one day at a time.

Chapter 8

Redefining Needs vs. Wants

Freedom Begins with Clarity

Have you ever bought something on a whim, only to feel buyer's remorse later? Or found yourself chasing the latest gadget, trend, or sale, thinking it would bring happiness, but it didn't? You're not alone. Most people struggle with the battle between "needs" and "wants," and that struggle is one of the biggest traps keeping them stuck in the broke lifestyle.

The good news? You don't have to live this way. When you learn to redefine your priorities, you'll discover the joy of spending with purpose—and the freedom of having more money for the things that truly matter.

1. The Impulse Trap: Why We Buy What We Don't Need

Impulse purchases are sneaky. They promise momentary happiness, but they come at a cost:

- **Lost Money:** Those "little" purchases add up. A $10 daily habit can cost you over $3,600 in a year!
- **Lost Peace:** Living paycheck-to-paycheck often stems from prioritizing wants over needs.
- **Lost Control:** When spending is driven by emotion, not intention, your finances control you, not the other way around.

The key to breaking free is recognizing that not all spending is bad—but *mindless* spending is.

---

2. Distinguishing Needs from Wants

Here's a simple test:

- **Needs** are essentials for survival and well-being. Think: housing, food, transportation, healthcare, and basic utilities.
- **Wants** are extras that bring enjoyment but aren't essential. Think: dining out, luxury items, or subscriptions you rarely use.

Sometimes the lines blur. For example, a car is a need if it gets you to work, but upgrading to a luxury model is a want.

Start by asking yourself these questions before spending:
1. Is this purchase necessary for my basic needs?
2. Will it add lasting value to my life, or is it a fleeting desire?
3. Does it align with my bigger financial goals?

---

3. Creating a Joyful Spending Plan

Budgeting isn't about cutting out all the fun—it's about spending intentionally. A "joyful spending" plan ensures you're putting money toward things that genuinely bring you happiness while keeping your long-term goals in sight.

Steps to Joyful Spending:

1. **Know Your Values:** What truly matters to you? Experiences with loved ones? Financial security? Personal growth? Spend on what aligns with your priorities.
2. **Set Limits for Wants:** Allocate a specific percentage of your budget for non-essentials. This creates boundaries while still allowing room for enjoyment.
3. **Plan for Fun:** Instead of impulsive spending, budget for fun purchases or experiences in advance. Anticipation makes them even more rewarding!

4. The Minimalist Mindset: Less Stuff, More Joy

Minimalism isn't about living with nothing; it's about living with *enough*. It's about freeing yourself from the clutter of unnecessary possessions to make room for what truly enriches your life.

Benefits of Minimalism:

- **Financial Freedom:** Fewer wants mean fewer expenses.
- **Emotional Freedom:** Owning less reduces stress and decision fatigue.
- **More Experiences:** Shifting your focus from things to experiences often leads to greater fulfillment.

Here's a challenge: Declutter one area of your life—your wardrobe, your kitchen, or your subscriptions. Sell, donate, or cancel what no longer serves you. Not only will you feel lighter, but you might even earn some extra cash!

5. Prioritizing Experiences Over Things

Research shows that experiences bring more lasting happiness than material possessions. Why?

- **Memories Last Longer:** You'll forget the thrill of a new gadget, but memories of a vacation or time with loved ones stick.
- **They Connect You to Others:** Experiences often involve shared moments, deepening relationships.

Next time you're tempted to buy something, ask yourself: "Would this money be better spent on an experience that aligns with my values?"

Action Step: Spend with Purpose

1. **Track Your Spending:** For one week, write down every purchase. At the end, categorize each as a need or a want.
2. **Create a Joy List:** Write down the top five things that bring you joy. Spend more on those and less on everything else.
3. **Say No:** The next time you're tempted to make an impulsive purchase, wait 24 hours. If it's still important after that, then consider it.

Freedom Is Found in Intention

Redefining your needs vs. wants isn't about deprivation—it's about liberation. It's about taking back control of your money and using it as a tool to build a life you truly love.

When you stop spending on things that don't matter, you create space for the things that do: financial stability, meaningful experiences, and the peace of knowing you're living with purpose.

The power to break free is already in your hands. Start today by choosing intention over impulse, purpose over pressure, and freedom over fleeting satisfaction. The result? A life that feels as good as it looks.

Chapter 9

Increasing Your Income Without Burning Out

The Secret to Growing Wealth Faster

When most people think about escaping the broke lifestyle, they focus solely on cutting back expenses. But here's the thing: there's only so much you can cut before you hit a wall. The real game-changer is increasing your income.

Imagine having the ability to save more, pay off debt faster, and invest in opportunities that create long-term security—all without sacrificing your sanity or burning yourself out. It's not just about working harder; it's about working smarter.

---

1. The Case for Earning More

Cutting back is essential, but it's only half the equation. When you earn more:

- You accelerate your financial goals exponentially.

- You create flexibility to enjoy life's pleasures without guilt.
- You break free from the constant stress of "just getting by."

Increasing your income doesn't mean hustling 24/7. It's about leveraging your time, skills, and creativity to maximize your earning potential while maintaining balance.

---

2. The Power of a Side Hustle or Skill Development

Side hustles aren't just trendy—they're powerful tools for breaking free from financial limitations. The key is finding something that aligns with your skills, interests, and availability.

Side Hustle Ideas:
- Freelancing: Writing, graphic design, web development, or virtual assistance.
- Selling Products: Start an Etsy shop, flip items online, or sell crafts.
- Tutoring or Teaching: Offer lessons in a subject, language, or skill you're proficient in.
- Driving or Delivery Services: Apps like Uber, DoorDash, or Instacart provide flexibility.

If you don't have time for a side hustle, focus on upgrading your skills. Online platforms like Coursera, Udemy, or LinkedIn Learning offer affordable courses to help you develop high-paying skills like coding, digital marketing, or project management.

---

3. Negotiating a Raise or Finding Higher-Paying Opportunities

Sometimes, the easiest way to increase your income is to maximize your current job's earning potential. If you've been delivering great results but haven't asked for a raise, now is the time to advocate for yourself.

Steps to Negotiate a Raise:
1. **Do Your Homework:** Research the average salary for your role in your area.
2. **Highlight Your Value:** List specific achievements and contributions you've made to the company.
3. **Time It Right:** Schedule a meeting after a successful project or during your performance review.
4. **Be Confident:** Believe in your worth and make a compelling case.

If your current job isn't providing growth opportunities, it may be time to explore higher-paying roles. Sometimes, switching companies or industries can significantly boost your salary.

4. The Magic of Passive Income

Passive income is the holy grail of financial freedom. It allows you to earn money with minimal ongoing effort, so you can build wealth without trading all your time.

Passive Income Ideas:
- **Real Estate:** Buy a rental property or invest through platforms like Fundrise.
- **Investing:** Start with index funds, dividend stocks, or robo-advisors.
- **Create Digital Products:** Write an eBook, design a course, or sell templates.
- **Affiliate Marketing:** Earn commissions by promoting products or services you love.

While passive income takes effort upfront, the long-term rewards are worth it. Start small and scale as you learn.

---

5. Avoiding Burnout While Increasing Income

Pursuing more income doesn't mean sacrificing your health or happiness. Here's how to maintain balance:

- **Set Boundaries:** Dedicate specific hours to your side hustle or skill development and stick to them.
- **Prioritize Rest:** Schedule downtime to recharge, and don't skip meals or sleep.

- **Celebrate Wins:** Recognize and reward yourself for milestones, no matter how small.

Remember, this journey isn't a sprint; it's a marathon. Pace yourself to stay consistent over the long haul.

Action Step: Plan Your Income Boost

1. **Identify One Opportunity:** Decide whether to start a side hustle, learn a new skill, or pursue a raise.
2. **Set a 30-Day Goal:** Outline a specific, actionable step—such as signing up for a course, pitching a client, or scheduling a meeting with your boss.
3. **Track Your Progress:** Measure your results weekly to stay motivated and adapt as needed.

Financial Freedom Starts with Earning More

You don't have to settle for scraping by. Increasing your income is the key to unlocking new possibilities, achieving financial stability, and building the life you've always dreamed of.

It's not about working harder—it's about working smarter. With a little creativity, focus, and determination, you can turn your skills and time into opportunities that change your financial future forever.

You've got the power to break free. Start now, and watch your life transform!

Chapter 10
Financial Systems That Work for You

Take the Stress Out of Money Management

Let's face it—managing money can feel overwhelming. Between paying bills, saving, investing, and tracking your progress, it's easy to lose track of what's happening with your finances. But here's the good news: you don't have to do it all manually or rely on willpower alone.

The secret? **Financial systems that work for you**—even when you're busy or feeling unmotivated. Systems remove guesswork, simplify decision-making, and ensure you're always moving toward your goals.

This chapter is all about designing financial systems that make managing money simple, stress-free, and sustainable.

1. Automating Your Financial Life

Automation is your best friend when it comes to staying on track. By automating key financial tasks, you ensure that your money is always working for you—without requiring constant attention.

What to Automate:
- **Savings:** Set up automatic transfers to a savings account every payday. Even $25 a week adds up over time.
- **Bills:** Use auto-pay for recurring expenses like rent, utilities, and subscriptions to avoid late fees.
- **Investments:** Most brokerages allow you to automate contributions to your 401(k), IRA, or brokerage account.

Why It Works:
- You remove the temptation to spend instead of save.
- You never miss a bill or payment, protecting your credit score.
- You build wealth consistently, even in small amounts.

Automation creates momentum, freeing up your energy for bigger financial decisions and goals.

2. Creating a Financial Calendar

A financial calendar helps you stay organized and proactive. Instead of reacting to financial surprises, you'll have a clear schedule for managing your money.

What to Include in Your Financial Calendar:

- **Weekly Check-Ins:** Review your spending and track your budget.
- **Monthly Check-Ins:** Assess your progress toward savings, debt repayment, and investment goals.
- **Quarterly Check-Ins:** Review your credit report, rebalance investments, and adjust your budget as needed.
- **Annual Check-In:** Evaluate your overall financial health and set goals for the coming year.

Use reminders on your phone or apps like Google Calendar to stay on schedule. By dedicating just 30 minutes a week, you'll feel more in control of your money.

---

3. Reviewing and Adjusting Your Financial Plan

Even the best financial plans need regular updates. Life changes—whether it's a new job, unexpected expenses, or personal milestones—require you to revisit your strategy and adjust as needed.

How to Review Your Plan:
1. **Revisit Your Goals:** Are they still relevant? Do you need to set new priorities?
2. **Track Your Progress:** Are you hitting savings and debt repayment milestones?
3. **Identify Bottlenecks:** What's slowing you down, and how can you fix it?

When to Adjust:
- **If Your Income Changes:** A raise or new job is a chance to increase savings or pay down debt faster.
- **If Your Expenses Change:** Adapt your budget to accommodate new expenses like a move, family growth, or health costs.
- **If Your Goals Evolve:** Shift your focus if you achieve one goal or discover new opportunities.

Regular reviews keep your financial plan aligned with your life, ensuring you stay on track no matter what comes your way.

---

4. Tools to Make Systems Easier

You don't have to manage everything on your own. Take advantage of financial tools and apps to simplify your systems:

- **Budgeting Apps:** Mint, YNAB (You Need a Budget), or EveryDollar.
- **Investment Platforms:** Acorns, Betterment, or Fidelity for automatic investing.
- **Savings Apps:** Digit or Qapital for setting aside small amounts without noticing.
- **Bill Management Tools:** Truebill or Prism to track and automate bill payments.

These tools save you time, reduce stress, and help you focus on what matters most—building a brighter financial future.

5. The Power of Consistency

The beauty of financial systems is that they make consistency easy. You don't have to make perfect decisions every day; the systems do the heavy lifting for you. Over time, those small, consistent efforts compound into massive financial wins.

Action Step: Build Your First System

1. **Automate One Thing:** Choose one financial task—saving, paying bills, or investing—and set up automation today.
2. **Create a Financial Calendar:** Schedule weekly and monthly check-ins to review your progress.

3. **Download a Tool or App:** Pick one app that can streamline your budgeting or saving process.

Set It and Prosper

Your financial success doesn't depend on endless effort or perfect discipline. It depends on smart systems that keep you moving forward, even when life gets busy.

By automating your finances, staying organized with a calendar, and regularly reviewing your plan, you'll create a foundation for lasting stability and growth.

You've got the tools, the knowledge, and the motivation to take control of your money. Start building your financial systems today—and watch how quickly your life transforms.

Chapter 11
Planning for the Future

Your Future Self Will Thank You

One of the greatest gifts you can give yourself is a solid financial plan for the future. Whether it's achieving financial freedom, retiring comfortably, or simply having peace of mind, planning for tomorrow starts with the steps you take today.

Planning isn't just about money—it's about giving yourself options, security, and the freedom to live life on your terms. Let's dive into how to create a roadmap for your financial future.

---

1. Setting Financial Goals That Stick

Goals give you direction. Without them, your money lacks purpose. The key is to set clear, actionable goals for the short, mid, and long term.

Short-Term Goals (1 Year or Less):
- Build an emergency fund.
- Pay off high-interest debt.
- Save for a specific purpose, like a vacation or new laptop.

Mid-Term Goals (1–5 Years):
- Save for a car, home, or further education.
- Eliminate all remaining consumer debt.
- Grow your investment portfolio.

Long-Term Goals (5+ Years):
- Retire with financial independence.
- Pay off your mortgage.
- Create a legacy through philanthropy or generational wealth.

The SMART Method:

Ensure your goals are **Specific, Measurable, Achievable, Relevant, and Time-Bound.** For example, instead of saying, "I want to save money," try: "I will save $10,000 in the next 12 months by setting aside $833 a month."

2. Retirement Planning: It's Never Too Early (or Late!)

Retirement may feel like a distant reality, but the earlier you start, the more powerful your financial momentum becomes. And if you're starting later, don't worry—it's never too late to take action.

Why Retirement Planning Matters:
- Social Security alone won't cut it.
- Compound interest favors time. Even small contributions grow significantly over decades.
- A financially secure retirement lets you focus on what matters most: family, travel, hobbies, or giving back.

How to Start:
- **401(k) or 403(b):** If your employer offers one, contribute enough to get the company match (it's free money!).
- **IRAs:** Open a Roth or Traditional IRA to take advantage of tax benefits.
- **Catch-Up Contributions:** If you're 50 or older, take advantage of higher contribution limits.
- **Invest Wisely:** Focus on diversified, low-cost index funds or target-date retirement funds.

Small Steps Add Up:

Even setting aside $50 a month can snowball into thousands over time. The key is consistency.

---

3. Future-Proofing Against Uncertainties

Life is full of surprises. The best way to protect your financial future is to prepare for the unexpected.

Emergency Fund:

Make sure you have 3–6 months' worth of expenses saved in an accessible account. This acts as a buffer for job loss, medical emergencies, or major repairs.

Insurance:

- **Health Insurance:** Ensure you're covered for medical emergencies.
- **Life Insurance:** If you have dependents, consider term life insurance to provide for them.
- **Disability Insurance:** Protect your income in case you're unable to work.

Estate Planning:

- Create a will to outline how your assets will be distributed.
- Designate beneficiaries for retirement accounts and insurance policies.

- Consider setting up a trust if you have significant assets or specific wishes for your estate.

Diversify Your Income:

Explore multiple income streams (e.g., investments, side hustles, or rental properties) to reduce dependence on any single source of income.

4. Staying Flexible with Your Plan

Financial planning isn't a one-and-done task. Your circumstances, goals, and priorities will evolve over time, so your plan should too.

When to Revisit Your Plan:
- After major life events (marriage, children, job change, etc.).
- Annually, to adjust for new goals or milestones.
- Anytime you feel your plan isn't serving you.

How to Adjust:
- Increase savings as your income grows.
- Shift investment strategies as you near retirement.
- Update your goals to reflect new aspirations or priorities.

5. Focus on Legacy, Not Just Wealth

Financial planning isn't just about numbers—it's about the impact you leave behind. What kind of life do you want to live? What kind of legacy do you want to create?

- **Generational Wealth:** Teach your children or loved ones about financial literacy.
- **Philanthropy:** Use your wealth to support causes you care about.
- **Personal Fulfillment:** Align your financial goals with your values to create a life of purpose and joy.

Action Step: Build Your Financial Roadmap

1. Write down one short-term, mid-term, and long-term goal.
2. Open or review a retirement account and commit to regular contributions.
3. Review your current insurance policies to identify any gaps.

Your Future Is in Your Hands

Planning for the future isn't about predicting what will happen—it's about preparing for what's possible. By setting goals, prioritizing retirement, and protecting yourself from uncertainties, you're building a foundation for a life of stability, security, and freedom.

Start today, no matter where you're starting from. The future you're dreaming of is closer than you think.

Chapter 12

Giving Back and Building Legacy

True Wealth Goes Beyond Dollars

You've worked hard to escape the cycle of financial struggle. You've learned to budget, save, invest, and plan for the future. Now it's time to talk about something bigger—what you do with your wealth to make a lasting impact. True wealth isn't just about having enough for yourself; it's about how you use your resources to elevate others, inspire change, and leave a meaningful legacy.

---

1. The Joy of Generosity

There's a unique joy that comes from giving. Generosity transforms lives—not just the lives of those you help but your own as well. Studies show that giving makes us happier, healthier, and more connected to others.

Why Giving Matters:
- **It multiplies impact:** Your success creates opportunities for others.
- **It reinforces gratitude:** Giving reminds you of how far you've come.
- **It builds community:** Generosity fosters connection and shared purpose.

Giving isn't just about writing checks. It's about finding ways to contribute that align with your passions and values. Whether it's supporting a cause you care about, mentoring someone in need, or volunteering your time, generosity has no limits.

---

2. Philanthropy with Purpose

Philanthropy doesn't have to be reserved for billionaires. You can make a significant difference at any income level by being intentional with your giving.

How to Give Strategically:
- **Identify Your Values:** What causes or communities are close to your heart?
- **Set a Giving Budget:** Just as you plan for savings and investments, allocate a portion of your income for giving.
- **Partner with Organizations:** Research charities or initiatives that align with your values and use

your resources wisely.

Even small acts of giving—buying lunch for someone in need, donating to a food bank, or supporting a local fundraiser—can have ripple effects that go far beyond the dollar amount.

---

3. Financial Mentoring: Share What You've Learned

One of the most powerful ways to give back is by teaching others what you've learned about breaking free from financial struggles. Your journey can inspire someone else to start theirs.

Ways to Mentor Others Financially:
- **Teach financial literacy:** Offer workshops or informal coaching on budgeting, saving, and investing.
- **Help someone in need:** Whether it's helping a family member get out of debt or showing a friend how to set up a budget, small steps can make a huge difference.
- **Lead by example:** Let your financial habits inspire others to take control of their own finances.

The more you empower others to take charge of their money, the more you amplify your impact.

---

4. Building a Legacy for Future Generations

True financial freedom is about more than your lifetime—it's about creating a foundation for future generations to thrive. Building a legacy isn't just about passing down money; it's about instilling values, teaching financial responsibility, and setting up systems that outlive you.

Steps to Build Your Legacy:

- **Teach Your Children (or Loved Ones):** Share your knowledge about budgeting, saving, and investing. Equip them with the tools they need to succeed.
- **Create a Will or Trust:** Ensure your assets are distributed in a way that reflects your wishes and provides for those you care about.
- **Invest in Education:** Contribute to scholarships, mentorships, or educational initiatives that help others achieve their dreams.

Your Legacy in Action:

Imagine a future where your children, grandchildren, or mentees carry forward the lessons you've learned. They'll remember not just the financial support you provided but the wisdom and values you passed down.

---

5. The Ripple Effect of Generosity

Generosity has a way of coming full circle. By giving to others, you not only contribute to their success but also create a ripple effect that touches countless lives.

Think about the mentors, teachers, or friends who helped you along your journey. Their support enabled you to get to where you are today. Now it's your turn to pay it forward.

Generosity can inspire:

- **A struggling friend** to believe in themselves.
- **A young mentee** to dream bigger.
- **A community** to come together for a shared purpose.

Your generosity has the power to spark hope and change lives.

Action Step: Define Your Legacy

1. Write down one cause or community you want to support.
2. Choose a specific way to give back this month—whether it's volunteering, donating, or mentoring.
3. Reflect on the impact you want to leave behind. What will your legacy be?

Your Greatest Impact Awaits

Breaking free from the broke lifestyle isn't just about building a better life for yourself. It's about using your financial freedom to lift others up, create opportunities, and leave the world a better place than you found it.

Your journey is proof that change is possible. By sharing your success, you multiply its impact. You're not just creating wealth—you're creating a movement. And that's a legacy worth leaving.

Conclusion

Breaking Free is a Journey, Not a Destination

You've Taken the First Step

Congratulations! You've just armed yourself with the tools, mindset, and strategies to break free from the paycheck-to-paycheck cycle and start building a brighter financial future. This book isn't just about information—it's about transformation.

Let's take a moment to reflect on the journey we've traveled together:

1. **Understanding the Real Cost of Staying Stuck:** You've learned how the broke lifestyle impacts every aspect of life—and why it's worth fighting to escape it.
2. **Identifying Common Traps:** From lifestyle inflation to social pressures, you've uncovered the obstacles holding you back.
3. **Facing the Emotional Side of Money:** You've explored the fears and mindsets that keep people

stuck and discovered how to reframe your relationship with money.
4. **Budgeting, Saving, and Debt-Free Living:** You now have a roadmap for managing your money wisely and building a foundation for financial stability.
5. **Small Investments, Big Wins:** Even small steps can grow into big results. You've learned how to start investing in a way that feels manageable and rewarding.
6. **Redefining Your Priorities:** By focusing on needs vs. wants, you've started to create a life centered on what truly matters to you.
7. **Increasing Income and Future-Proofing Your Finances:** You're ready to take control of your earning potential and set yourself up for long-term security.
8. **Giving Back and Building a Legacy:** True wealth isn't just about you. It's about the impact you leave on the world and the people you inspire along the way.

Start Today, Not Someday

Here's the truth: the path to financial freedom isn't always easy, but it's worth it. Every small step you take moves you closer to a life of stability, opportunity, and peace of mind.

Will it take discipline? Yes. Will there be challenges? Absolutely.
But the rewards? They're priceless.

Imagine what it will feel like to:

- Stop worrying about unexpected expenses.
- Say yes to opportunities without hesitation.
- Build a life that reflects your values and dreams.

It all starts with the choice you make today.

The Journey Is Yours to Take

Breaking free isn't a one-time decision. It's a series of daily choices. Some days will feel like victories; others may feel like setbacks. But no matter what, keep moving forward.

You are not alone in this journey. Thousands of others are also choosing to break free, rewrite their stories, and build a better future. The most important thing is to start —and never stop.

Your Next Step

Close this book, and take one action today. It doesn't matter if it's small or bold. Just start. Create your first budget. Set up your emergency fund. Make a plan to tackle your debt. Reach out to someone who can mentor you.

The difference between those who stay stuck and those who break free isn't knowledge—it's action.

Your Future Is Worth It

This isn't just about escaping the broke lifestyle. It's about creating a life where you thrive, where you can dream without limits, and where you leave behind a legacy of abundance and impact.

Your journey starts now. Take the first step. Your future self will thank you.

Bonus Materials

Worksheets and Templates

These tools will help you put the lessons of this book into action. Download them, print them, or recreate them in a notebook—whatever works best for you.

1. **Budget Tracker**
    - Income (monthly):
        - Main source: _____
        - Side hustles: _____
    - Expenses (monthly):
        - Housing: _____
        - Utilities: _____
        - Food: _____
        - Transportation: _____
        - Other: _____
    - Total: _____
    - Difference (Income - Expenses): _____

    Use this to identify areas where you can cut back and redirect toward your goals.

2. **Debt Repayment Plan**

- List your debts:
    - Lender: _____
    - Balance: _____
    - Interest Rate: _____
    - Minimum Payment: _____
- Choose your method:
    - Snowball (smallest balance first).
    - Avalanche (highest interest rate first).
- Track progress monthly:
    - Amount paid: _____
    - Remaining balance: _____

3. **Emergency Fund Goal Sheet**

    - Goal: Save $_____
    - Monthly savings target: _____
    - Completion date: _____

Reflection Questions

Take a few moments to answer these questions and gain clarity about your financial journey.

1. **What is your biggest financial fear?**
   Write it down: _____
   Reflect: How does this fear hold you back, and what steps can you take to overcome it?

2. **What would financial freedom mean to you?**
   Write it down: _____
   Reflect: Imagine a day when money is no longer a source of stress. What would that feel like?

3. **What habit or mindset do you need to change first?**
   Write it down: _____
   Reflect: What action can you take this week to start that change?

Resources Section

These books, podcasts, and websites will keep you motivated and informed on your journey to financial freedom.

Books:

- *The Total Money Makeover* by Dave Ramsey
- *Rich Dad Poor Dad* by Robert Kiyosaki
- *Your Money or Your Life* by Vicki Robin
- *I Will Teach You to Be Rich* by Ramit Sethi

Podcasts:

- *Afford Anything* by Paula Pant
- *The Dave Ramsey Show*
- *BiggerPockets Money Podcast*
- *ChooseFI*

Websites:

- NerdWallet (Budgeting and saving tools).
- Investopedia (Financial education).
- BiggerPockets (Real estate investing).
- Mint (Budgeting app).

Your Next Step

Use these tools to take action immediately. Remember: Progress, not perfection, is the goal. Celebrate each small victory as you move closer to breaking free from the broke lifestyle!

www.ingramcontent.com/pod-product-compliance
Lightning Source LLC
Chambersburg PA
CBHW070352230526
45471CB00006B/2532